# Rhyr

Ayme Friggle

BookLeaf
Publishing

Rhymes of Life © 2023 Ayme Friggle

Presentation by *BookLeaf Publishing*

Web: www.bookleafpub.com

E-mail: info@bookleafpub.com

ISBN: 9789357442992

First edition 2023

*For my two children, Marissa and Brandon,
who keep me busy and inspired.*

*For my Mom who has asked for decades that I
get my poetry published. Here you go!*

*To my Dad who has always been the best man
in my life. Thank you for being the best Dad
and a best friend.*

# ACKNOWLEDGEMENT

Thank you to my favorite English teachers who encouraged and elevated when it was needed most.
Mr. Campbell
Mrs. Weimmer

A great teacher can impact more than just their students by starting a ripple that changes the course of those connected to them.

# PREFACE

I started writing poetry at age five.

I have always loved to watch the world, people, animals, events and just everything. I observe, analyze, soak it in and spit back out my interpretations of it all in written words, in poetry.

The world is poetry in motion.

It really truly is.

We live poetry.

We experience poetry.

Poetry is the expression of life's inspiration.

I hope you find a connection within these pages.

# Coming of the Night

I walk along the path
A long road stretched behind
Not realizing how far I've gone
Nor what I longed to find.
The road was warm on my feet
With flowers grown alongside
In places where the wind was calm
And the sun had always shined.
There was mud thick in puddles
Where rain had poured
And some dried between my toes
A constant reminder of hardships endured.
This place I am at now
I can't really be sure
How much time I have to continue
Or if I have any more.

The road has divided,
And I walked down one side.
A feeling of peace has come over me
As I leave that world behind.
I may not know what could have been
If I stayed to the right
But it won't stop the lives of others
Nor the Coming of the Night.

# Perfection

Misty light, deep black sky
The Heavens' in clear view tonight.
Crisp clean air - pure and cool.
Shadows fall in pale moonlight.
Behind the trees,
The mountains fade.
Below the cliff,
A chattering sea.
A purple outline ascends to the peak,
and black water runs deep.
So peaceful and still,
As the waves dance slowly with joy
Looking up at their audience,
The beholder in a trance.
Beauty, natural -
untouched by Demons.
The hands that corrode have not yet grabbed
The perfect seasons of an undisturbed land.

# Senseless

Waiting in silence
Wishing I knew
how could I be so blind
to the pain I feel from you?
My eyes open wide
but never once saw evil,
only love and happiness,
now feeling so pitiful.
When did my sight decide
to leave me without warning?
The tears I'm crying,
covering my vision,
Being oblivious to heartache,
my eyes deceived me too.
Left to lie in the bed I make,
Falling in love so unsuspecting,
But starting to realize,
I can't handle the outcome,
No matter what I tried,
Being left blind, I am also deaf and dumb.

# A Fine Line of Trust

What can you call trust?
There's a fine line to define
When someone betrays your confidence
When to forgive, what not to forget,
Loyalty is shown to an extent.
When is it wrong if the rules are bent?
Can you move on and trust just the same -
or is an understanding broken and hostility as
the remain?
If you remember, does the past reoccur?
Does the betrayal ever cool down,
or will emotions continue to stir?
When do you know trust is lost -
and at what cost?
Can you determine how to decide?
Trust has a fine line to define.

# Hourglass

Time drags on when I have
    no patience
But goes so rapidly when
    I'm enjoying it.
The days go by so slow
    when I count them down
But race by when I'm
    not ready to let them end.
The weeks just creep by like a
    turtle's stride when there's nothing to do
But when I'm busy,  I hardly have time
    to see them go.
The months never end while
    I await a holiday
But disappear before
    I blink my eyes.
The years of my childhood took so long
    to let me grow and taste adulthood
But now I age so quickly
    and years pass as days.

# Body n' Soul

Let's take a journey
Just you and I
We'll sleep tonight
and sneak by
those who keep us here
You shall leave through the mind
and I will drift outside.
Dream of where we will go
And that is where I will fly.
You can watch me
So we'll be together.
When I get back and reunite,
You can awake and decide,
If we will return once again,
to live away from where we escape
and find peace and happiness
permanently in a new place.
So when our trip is completed,
it will be all we needed.

# My Pictures of You

I have just so many pictures of you
I kept every one.
I look at all my pictures of you
And see your laughter, all our fun.
I hold my pictures of you,
While watching your smile.
My pictures of you are all I have
to remember that style.
I keep your pictures in a box,
not nearly full of dust.
I look at them so much,
I'm surprised they're not faded away,
Like You
Maybe someday I'll put away
My pictures of you,
If you come back to take their place.
But for now all I can do,
is look at these pictures of
Memories I can't erase.
In my pictures of you,
I see happiness in your face.
And until I see you,
I will save my pictures
And my memories too.

# Thief of Hearts

He doesn't even realize
Nor see what he has done
He causes the tears pouring from my eyes
For unknown to him, my heart he has won.

A Thief of Hearts
He is the bait that hooked my love
So much mending and tearing apart
But I'm in too deep to just give up.

I've lost my senses
Reality has left my mind
I can not forget what he means to me
Life without his love, I do not want to find.

A Thief of Hearts
He is heavily armed
Disguised with saddened smiles
His weapon - abundant charm.

A smooth operator
He slithered into my dreams
Of my confusion, he is the creator
I am the center of his schemes.

A Thief of Hearts
Mine is captive in his grasp
Being worn down by an emotional tug of war
I'm not sure how long my sanity will last.

This Thief of Hearts
If he has deceived my mind
All of his lines I have bought
Within his trap, I've been caught.

# Untitled

Look at me,
A mere tree,
So saddened by losing my leaves,
A part of me.
Grown so close, within so long,
But now they are all gone.
I am bare.
Coldly I stare,
At the pine,
That sits safe all the time,
Her stems protected and loved,
Jealousy is not enough
to satisfy me now,
Alone, with part of me ripped out.

# Hope

I never thought to tell you then,
How much I love you so.
Now I search for you my friend,
And fear you may never know.

I have only words that can not begin to describe
What we have seen in that New York sky.
The gruesome attack that has claimed so many
lives,
And caused the tears we cry.

We sit here with anger, fear and pain,
Feeling helpless and unsure of what to do.
Our lives have forever been changed,
As we try desperately to face the news.

Others lash out in rage at the evil,
But we stand united with this common bond of
someone we knew.
We share memories and moments that reveal
How our lives will be forever touched by you.

Whether years, months, or just one day,
We all have precious times to call our own.
Times with you we may never get again,
But together, we will never be alone.

The world has come together,
We will not let this be in vain.
Your friends are bound forever,
Our love and hope remains.

For Chris Traina and those that love him, written
September 14, 2001.
It was later confirmed that Chris was a victim in
the towers on 9/11/01.

# MAYBE I KNOW

I am not sure why
I am not sure how
Maybe the answers would not satisfy me
Maybe I am not ready to know just now.
I am not sure where you've gone
I am not sure what you've seen
Maybe I want to believe in my own mind
Maybe it's a better scene.
I am not sure what I feel
I am not sure if you knew
Maybe you waited to hear me say
Maybe you hear me now: I love you.
I am not good at this pain
I am not good at this at all
Maybe you are still around to help me through
Maybe we will meet again after all.
I am sure that I miss you so
I am sure that my heart aches without you here
Maybe you are happy and free
Maybe you are still very near.
I am sure I will always cherish the time with you
I am sure I will hold you close in my memory
Maybe I will take comfort in believing
Maybe you are still with me.

# Portraits

On my canvas
the paint is so permanent
No matter how hard I wish
I can't erase my mistakes.
The pictures aren't always perfect
But I don't always remember
the errors I make.
Each day, a new picture
of my life is created -
Changing rapidly as I go on.
Times I've stopped and debated
Whether or not I was wrong.
People enter and leave my view
And some never stay long,
But everyone paints their own canvas,
Displaying their works in the gallery of the mind
Someday the final canvas will be hung
and others will grieve after the last
But no matter how we say goodbye,
We can never go back to the past.

# Just for a Moment

I remember two years ago
When you smiled so warmly
I never thought you'd ever know
How much that smile meant to me.

I'd stare from every room
And try to get close
In frustration I'd assume
You'd think I just impose

I remember the night I said goodbye
And you left for school
I began to cry
But wanted to keep my heart from you.

The final hug, I couldn't let go
I grasped so tightly
And reluctantly lost control
You held me silently.

I said I had loved you
Knowing your care not as great for me
My dreams began to come true
As my heart was struck with reality.

The first and last kiss you gave
Ended within minutes of final say
All that's left are memories saved
As I watched you walk away.

Now it's been so long
But I'll never forget
How, for one moment I belonged
With feelings equally met.

# Revelation

Prophecy of Heaven
revoke me of guilt
For I repent
everyone else's sins
Predict my Fate
I beg you
to control this destiny
Join me in my undertaking
of ultimate delight
Release me of their Wickedness
So others view the Real Me
I am tired of being my only defense
Give me strength to overcome
All the pain from being misjudged
I need to be extricated from this life
    as someone new.

# Comforter

Come my love, rest your weary feet
Sit upon my lap,
I will protect you through your nap.
Just close your eyes, lean against my heart
the beat will calm your nerves
And sooth with hypnotic art.
Take my hand in your grasp,
And squeeze the pain into me
I will bear it until I bleed,
if the case may be.
So gentle I will cradle you,
Like you've never felt before.
Forever in my arms,
You shall cry no more.
Smiling while you dream,
My thoughts wander at the sight.
Sleep my love, warm and safe,
in the coldness of the night.

# Seperation

A waterfall that glides gently down a mountain
side
reflects a peaceful sight
Just like the vision of you
when I close my eyes.
Morning dew trickles off a withering flower,
fading into the soil
Like the tears that poured from
your shiny brown eyes
Branches snap underneath my feet
screaming in agony
As your voice had sounded
when I turned away
The cool breeze rushes through
chilling my bones
Just as my body quivered
in your desperate last grasp
The sun begins to slither down to set
Just as I hope you may someday do
Without me, once again.

# Conflicting Thoughts

emotions and thoughts
of love and pain
devotions, destructions,
heartbreaks, again and again.
affectionate glances
feelings of needing you
desperate chances
to keep the spark,
a flame of passion
burning in my soul,
for someone so near,
yet an impossible goal.
why yearnings are so strong
I don't know
my thoughts are always of you
where ever I go.

# Blinding Temptation

Temptation dangles in such close grasp,
Take what you can before they take it back.
Flames lit around her body,
She kept them burning all night.
He tried to look, but couldn't see
Only heat penetrated into his eyes.
As she said "Don't look into the fire
'cause love can make you blind."

Just like the road to Hell,
Paved with desire -
An eternal yearning,
She was the spark leading to fire.
With the flick of her match,
she cast a spell deep inside.

She wouldn't touch - he wanted to try.
He feared being scorched,
but she hypnotized his mind.
She said, "Don't look into the fire
'cause love can make you blind."

Just like the road to Hell,
paved with desire.
An eternal yearning,

She was the spark leading to fire
With the flick of her match,
She cast a spell deep inside.

He couldn't understand
What powers she possessed,
His questions received no answer -
He was obsessed.
And she said, "Don't stare into the fire,
'cause love can make you blind."

Just like the road to Hell,
Paved with desire,
An eternal yearning -
She was the spark leading to fire.
With the flick of her match,
She cast a spell deep inside.

# My Grieving Heart

Tears I shed today are a tribute,
A reflection of personal sadness.
My own selfish wish of wanting you here
I know I am powerless,
And time with you just memories
of love, joy and happiness.
But I can not help but reflect
On all the greatness you possessed.
So many lives you have blessed.
Like others I love who have left,
I will always remember you too.
Yes, right now with deep sadness,
But always and forever with great fondness.
You, my loving partner and friend,
Will someday be with me again.
So let me cry for you for awhile
Let my frustration and pain take its place,
For healing will come at a timely pace.
And my love with continue each day,
Because your love shall guide my way.

# All Along

I could look into your eyes
And wonder where the time has gone.
To see you now and hear your cries,
I guess I knew it all along.

Those eyes still glisten when you smile.
The bond between us remains strong.
I thought of you all the while,
I guess I knew it all along.

When we parted, I felt the same.
Now when I hear our song,
Memories of love replace the pain.
I guess I knew it all along.

Now the future we'll find together,
The past mistakes are buried and gone.
Our new ties won't sever.
I guess I knew it all along.

Printed in the USA
CPSIA information can be obtained
at www.ICGtesting.com
LVHW011907300923
759798LV00005B/301